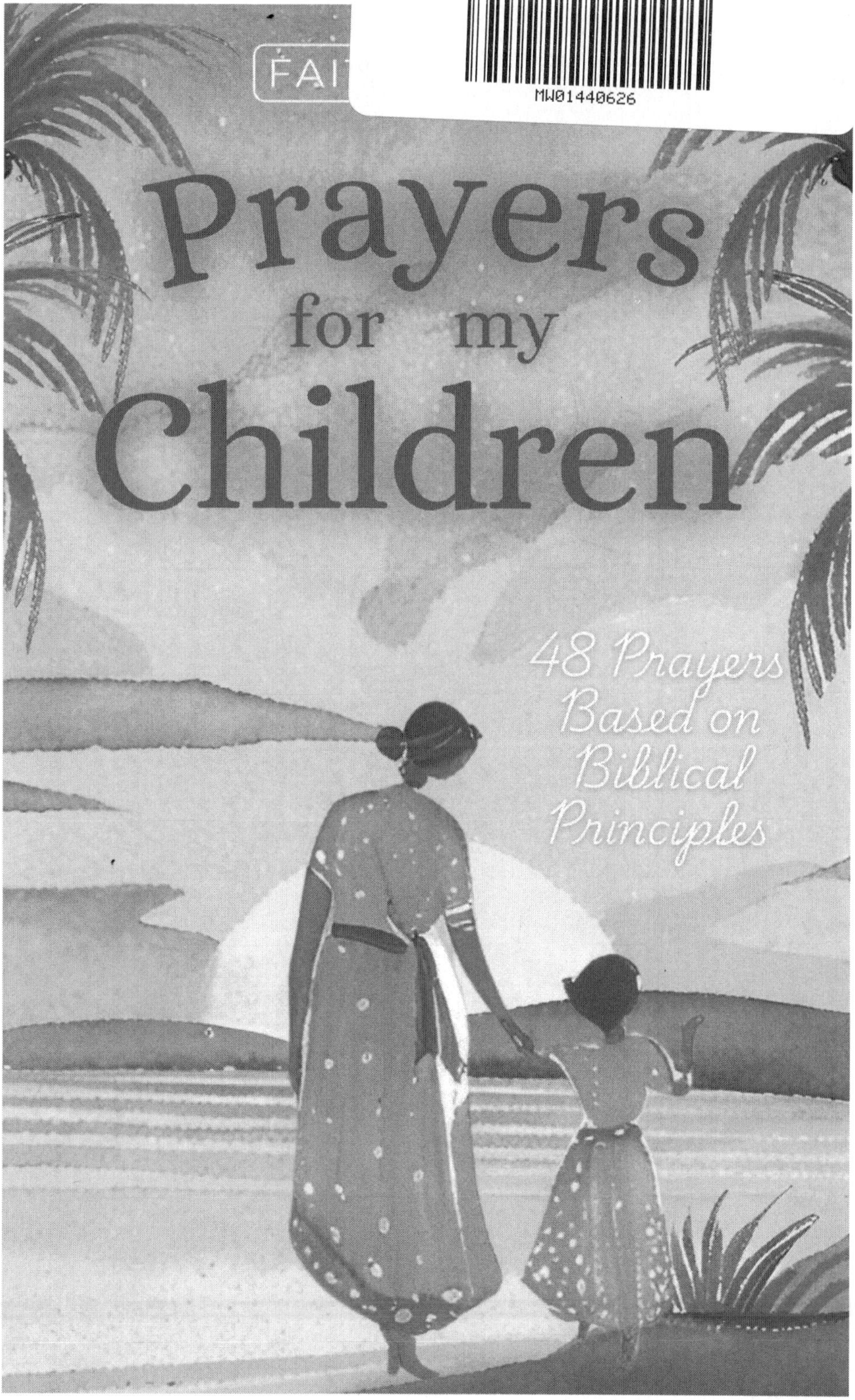

Prayers for my Children

48 Prayers Based on Biblical Principles

Prayers for my Children

48 Prayers Based on Biblical Principles

FAITH LABS

THANK YOU
for your purchase!

Grow your faith with a **free** bonus book included in *every* purchase.

GET IT NOW

Every purchase comes with a free bonus book download.

FAITH LABS

Prayers for My Children
48 Prayers Based on Biblical Principles

Copyright 2025

FAITH LABS

All rights reserved. No part of this publication may be reproduced, stored or transmitted in any form or by any means, electronic, mechanical, photocopying, recording, scanning, or otherwise without written permission from the publisher. It is illegal to copy this book, post it to a website, or distribute it by any other means without permission.

Disclaimers and Terms of Use: The publisher and author do not warrant or represent that the contents within are accurate and disclaim all warranties and is not liable for any damages whatsoever. Although all attempts were made to verify information, they do not assume any responsibility for errors, omissions, or contrary interpretation of the subject matter contained within as perceived slights of peoples, persons, organizations are unintentional and information contained within should not be used as a source of legal, business, accounting, financial, or other professional advice. Publisher and author has no responsibility for the persistence or accuracy of URLs for external or third-party Internet Websites referred to in this publication and does not guarantee that any content on such Websites is, or will remain, accurate or appropriate.

Product names, logos, brands, and other trademarks featured or referred to within this publication are the property of their respective trademark holders and are not sponsored, approved, licensed, or endorsed by any of their licensees or affiliates.

6 PRAYERS FOR MY CHILDREN

Table of Contents

INTRODUCTION 9
PRAYING FOR YOUR CHILD'S FAITH 15
PRAYING FOR YOUR CHILD'S HEALTH 25
PRAYING FOR YOUR CHILD'S RELATIONSHIPS 35
PRAYING FOR YOUR CHILD'S FUTURE 45
PRAYING FOR YOUR CHILD'S EDUCATION 55
PRAYING FOR YOUR CHILD'S EMOTIONAL
WELL-BEING 65
ENCOURAGEMENT TO CONTINUE PRAYING 75
ABOUT US 83

INTRODUCTION

Everyone has different experiences when it comes to growing up. Everyone had different parents who all had different beliefs, practices, and cultures, and thus, no one's childhood is ever really the same as another person's. What is common in most people's upbringing is being taught by their parents to keep their faith in God. From a young age, a child is taught by their parents to pray to God, to give their thanks to God, and sometimes to even ask forgiveness from God.

A child, learning how to have faith in God from a young age, will have a spiritual foundation, and with a foundation that is built on being faithful to God, one can only imagine just how faithful they are to become once they are older. Having faith in God also allows the child to have a moral compass, which would allow them to distinguish right from wrong at an early age. Along with the practices of a

Christian upbringing, a child will eventually develop virtues such as honesty, kindness, compassion, forgiveness, and love.

A belief in God means that a child would also believe in the eternal life that is promised to them, when following the Christian faith. In line with this, teaching children about the love of God helps them understand that there is more to this life than material possessions and achievements that are not beneficial in the long run. Instead, having faith and belief in God helps them understand that loving others and sharing what physical blessings they already own would be more beneficial than keeping them for themselves.

Children growing up with passionate and kind adults around them is also very important. When raising children to be faithful to God, they are usually brought along with their parents to churches and Sunday Services, where they are also able to meet other families who believe in the same faith; and can even connect with children whose parents are teaching them the same values. Doing this allows the child to grow up in a community that prioritizes loving and supporting each other, the way God intended for them to do so. This also instills a strong sense of community in a child, which would hopefully guide them into showing love, kindness, and compassion to those around them who are in need.

The best part about a child growing up in an environment that is full of faith is that they are most likely to share their own childhood experiences with their own children in the future. This would lead to a new generation of young people who would share the same faith, and who would also be able to spread the word of God. These children would then, just like their parents, continue spreading the word of God, making more people believe in God as well. All of this would ultimately lead to more people showing love and kindness to others, ultimately creating a never-ending cycle of love, joy, and faith.

Proverbs 22:6 (KJV)

"Train up a child in the way he should go: and when he is old, he will not depart from it."

1
PRAYING FOR YOUR CHILD'S FAITH

Prayer for Your Child to Have Guidance

"Trust in the LORD with all thine heart; and lean not unto thine own understanding. In all thy ways acknowledge him, and he shall direct thy paths."

Proverbs 3:5-6 (KJV)

Prayer

Dear God, please guide my child in following the responsibilities that have been entrusted to them. Guide my child in all that they do so that they may take the path that is righteously good and honorable. Please guide them to make smart decisions and good choices that would honor you. Amen.

Reflection Question

How can your child learn to trust God's guidance in their daily life? How can you teach them to acknowledge God in everything they do?

Prayer for Your Child's Strength

> *"Fear thou not; for I am with thee: be not dismayed; for I am thy God: I will strengthen thee; yea, I will help thee; yea, I will uphold thee with the right hand of my righteousness."*
>
> Isaiah 41:10 (KJV)

Prayer

Dear Heavenly Father, I beg of you to give my child strength whenever they feel small, weak, or afraid. Please give them the strength to trust in you, and in me. Please give me the strength to remember that You and I are always with them no matter where they go or what they do. Amen.

Reflection Question

How can you teach them to rely on God's strength in times of difficulty? How would you teach them that knowing God is with them can give them courage?

Prayer for Your Child's Gratefulness

"In everything give thanks: for this is the will of God in Christ Jesus concerning you."

1 Thessalonians 5:18 (KJV)

Prayer

Dear Holy Father, I want to thank You for everything I have in my life. I would like Your help in teaching my child to always be grateful to You for having parents/guardians that care for them, for having food to eat, and for the clothes and shelter that keep them warm. Amen.

Reflection Question

What are some specific things your child can be grateful for today? How can you teach your child to develop a habit of expressing gratitude to God and others?

Prayer for Your Child to be Forgiven

"Forbearing one another, and forgiving one another, if any man has a quarrel against any: even as Christ forgave you, so also do ye."

Colossians 3:13 (KJV)

Prayer

Dear Holy Father, I want to thank You for everything I have in my life. I would like Your help in teaching my child to always be grateful to You for having parents/guardians that care for them, for having food to eat, and for the clothes and shelter that keep them warm. Amen.

Reflection Question

What are some specific things your child can be grateful for today? How can you teach your child to develop a habit of expressing gratitude to God and others?

Prayer for Your Child to be Protected

"For he shall give his angels charge over thee, to keep thee in all thy ways."

Psalm 91:11 (KJV)

Prayer

Lord, please keep my child safe from all types of harm. Please make sure our homes are locked tight and are always secure. Please keep my child safe from evil and temptation so that my child also may not harm others. Protect my child from those who intend to do them harm so that they may continue being happy and healthy and continue to grow in your image. Amen.

Reflection Question

How does knowing that God protects and watches over you bring you peace? How can you develop a stronger sense of trust in God's care and protection?

Prayer for Your Child's Love

"Beloved, let us love one another: for love is of God; and everyone that loveth is born of God, and knoweth God."

1 John 4:7 (KJV)

Prayer

Dear God, I ask for your help in teaching my child how to love others in the same way that You have loved them. I would like my child to share the love that You share with us with everyone around them, including our other family members, my child's friends, and even their teachers. Amen.

Reflection Question

How can you demonstrate God's love to those around you and your child? What are some practical ways to show kindness and compassion to others in order to show your child the way to show kindness and compassion?

Prayer for Your Child's Wisdom

> *"If any of you lack wisdom, let him ask of God, that giveth to all men liberally, and upbraideth not; and it shall be given him."*
>
> James 1:5 (KJV)

Prayer

Dear Heavenly Father, I ask you to give my child wisdom. Please allow them this so that they are able to make good choices for themself and for the people around them. Please give them wisdom so that they can decide for themself instead of blindly following their friends and classmates. Please help them understand what is wrong and right so that they do not bring you shame. Amen.

Reflection Question

How can seeking God's wisdom help your child in their daily life? In what areas of their life do they need wisdom and understanding?

Prayer for Your Child's Obedience

"If ye love me, keep my commandments."

John 14:15 (KJV)

Prayer

Dear Heavenly God, please guide my child so that they may continue to be Your obedient child. Please guide them and give them the strength they need to remind themselves to always obey the Ten Commandments so that they may continue to honor you. Please also give them the obedience to always follow me, and their teachers. Amen.

Reflection Question

How does obedience to God's commandments demonstrate your child's love for Him? What can your child do to align their actions with God's will and teachings?

2

PRAYING FOR YOUR CHILD'S HEALTH

Prayer for Physical Healing

> *"For I will restore health unto thee, and I will heal thee of thy wounds, saith the LORD."*
>
> Jeremiah 30:17 (KJV)

Prayer

Dear Heavenly Father, I ask you to completely heal and restore the body of my child. Please allow Your healing power to flow through their bodies so that their health may be completely restored. Please help them so that my child will be able to smile without pain. Please give them the strength to keep fighting. Amen.

Reflection Question

How does knowing that God can restore health give you and your child hope? How can you and your child trust God's healing process, even in difficult times?

Prayer for Emotional Well-being

> *"The righteous cry, and the LORD heareth, and delivereth them out of all their troubles."*
>
> Psalm 34:17 (KJV)

Prayer

Dear Heavenly God, please bring peace of mind and comfort to my child's heart and mind. Please give them the courage and strength they need to face and fight through the pain that they are feeling. Please cover them with Your love so that they are reminded of Your loving and caring presence. Amen.

Reflection Question

How can your child find solace and peace in God's presence? What steps can you take to support a child's emotional well-being?

Prayer for Strength and Energy

> "He giveth power to the faint; and to them that have no might he increaseth strength."
>
> Isaiah 40:29 (KJV)

Prayer

Dear Heavenly Father, please grant my child renewed strength. Please give them boundless energy so that they may continue to fill this world You have created with joy and laughter. Please fill them with vitality and happiness to enjoy each day of their lives with enthusiasm and laughter. Amen.

Reflection Question

How can you and your child rely on God's strength in times of weakness? How can a child use their strength and energy to serve and glorify God?

Prayer for Protection from Illness

> *"There shall no evil befall thee, neither shall any plague come nigh thy dwelling."*
>
> Psalm 91:10 (KJV)

Prayer

Dear Heavenly Father, please shield my child from all of the sickness and disease that come with this beautiful world that we live in. Please surround my child with Your divine protection and grace until the day they return to Your loving arms. Please keep them strong and healthy. Amen.

Reflection Question

How can you trust in God's protection of your child during times of widespread illness? How can your child take practical steps to maintain good health?

Prayer for Healing Relationships

"Let not mercy and truth forsake thee: bind them about thy neck; write them upon the table of thine heart: So shalt thou find favour and good understanding in the sight of God and man."

Proverbs 3:3-4 (KJV)

Prayer

Dear Heavenly Father, I please ask you to heal any broken or strained relationships that exist in my child's life. Please restore love, understanding, and peace in my child's life and in the people around them. Please guide them so that they may continue to get along well with others and share with them the word of Your love. Amen.

Reflection Question

How can you show mercy and truth in your relationships with others in order to show your child? What steps can your child take to promote reconciliation and forgiveness?

Prayer for Sound Sleep

> *"I will both lay me down in peace and sleep: for thou, LORD, only makest me dwell in safety."*
>
> Psalm 4:8 (KJV)

Prayer

Dear Heavenly Lord, please grant my child a peaceful and restful sleep for the rest of their life. Please allow their mind to be calmed down and quieted so that he may close their eyes without having to worry about anything else. Please grant them a good night's sleep every night until the end of their days. Amen.

Reflection Question

How can you and your child find peace and rest in God's presence? What bedtime routine or practices can help your child have a good night's sleep?

Prayer for Healthy Habits

"What? know ye not that your body is the temple of the Holy Ghost which is in you, which ye have of God, and ye are not your own? For ye are bought with a price: therefore glorify God in your body, and in your spirit, which are God's."

1 Corinthians 6:19-20 (KJV)

Prayer

Dear Heavenly Father, please guide my child into making healthy and smart choices for themselves, their body, and their mind. Please guide them into developing productive and healthy habits that would promote the longevity of their life and their well-being. Please guide them so that they may continue these habits until the end of their days. Amen.

Reflection Question

How can you and your child honor God with your bodies through healthy habits? What healthy choices can your child incorporate into their daily routine?

Prayer for God's Peace and Presence

> *"And the peace of God, which passeth all understanding, shall keep your hearts and minds through Christ Jesus."*
>
> Philippians 4:7 (KJV)

Prayer

Dear God, please fill my child with Your peace. Please assure my child that Your loving and guiding presence is a constant that will be there for them for the rest of their life. Please provide them with a deep sense of security and well-being so that they may continue to live a long, happy, and prosperous life the way you intend for them to do so. Amen.

Reflection Question

How can you all experience God's peace that surpasses all understanding? What can your child do to cultivate a sense of God's presence in their daily life?

3
PRAYING FOR YOUR CHILD'S RELATIONSHIPS

Prayer for Healthy Friendships

"He that walketh with wise men shall be wise: but a companion of fools shall be destroyed."

Proverbs 13:20 (KJV)

Prayer

Dear God, I ask you to please bless my child with friendships that would support them and make them happy. I ask you to please guide my child into finding friends who also honor you the same way my child honors you. Please surround them with friends who would encourage their faith and share their values. Amen.

Reflection Question

How can you guide your child in choosing wise friends? What qualities should your child look for in their friendships?

Prayer for Sibling Relationship

> *"Behold, how good and how pleasant it is for brethren to dwell together in unity!"*
>
> Psalm 133:1 (KJV)

Prayer

Heavenly Father, please guide my children into always being there for each other from childhood and even all the way until adulthood. Please remind them that family is always there to support each other no matter what. Please guide them back to each other no matter what petty fights or arguments they share during the years they grow up. Amen.

Reflection Question

How can you encourage a spirit of unity and cooperation among your children? What steps can your children take to strengthen their sibling relationships?

Prayer for Parent-Child Bond

> *"Train up a child in the way he should go: and when he is old, he will not depart from it."*
>
> Proverbs 22:6 (KJV)

Prayer

Dear God, I ask You to please help me deepen the bond that is between me and my child. Help me to understand my child so that I may guide them to the best of my abilities. Please also fill my child with understanding so that they realize I must do what I have to do because I love them. Please fill our relationship with respect, trust, and connection. Amen.

Reflection Question

How can you actively invest in building a strong relationship with your child? In what ways can you demonstrate love and understanding in your interactions with your child?

Prayer for Teachers and Mentors

> *"The rich ruleth over the poor, and the borrower is servant to the lender."*
>
> Proverbs 22:7 (KJV)

Prayer

Dear Heavenly Father, please guide the teachers and mentors who are in my child's life. Please guide them so that they may be able to teach my child in the best way possible. Please give them the patience and understanding necessary in order to successfully teach a child. Please also fill my child with gratitude so that they may understand how much work their teachers and mentors put into their work. Amen.

Reflection Question

How can you support and appreciate the teachers and mentors in your child's life? How can your child benefit from the wisdom and guidance of their teachers and mentors?

Prayer for Peer Pressure

"Be not deceived: evil communications corrupt good manners."

1 Corinthians 15:33 (KJV)

Prayer

Dear God, please give my child the strength to not give in to peer pressure. Please give them the courage to stand up to those they believe are acting negatively. Please also give them the courage to spread Your love to them so that they may see the error in their own ways. Help these children make better choices that would honor You. Amen.

Reflection Question

How can you equip your child to navigate peer pressure with wisdom and discernment? What are some healthy strategies your child can use to resist negative influences?

Prayer for Forgiveness and Reconciliation

> *"Forbearing one another, and forgiving one another, if any man has a quarrel against any: even as Christ forgave you, so also do ye."*
>
> Colossians 3:13 (KJV)

Prayer

Dear Heavenly Father, please teach my child the importance of forgiveness. Please guide them into forgiving and reconciling with someone who has wronged them and give them another chance. Please guide my child into being a person of peace and not of anger or hate. Give them the wisdom to be able to mend broken relationships. Amen.

Reflection Question

How can you model forgiveness and reconciliation in your own relationships? What steps can your child take to initiate reconciliation with others?

Prayer for Respect and Kindness

> *"Therefore all things whatsoever ye would that men should do to you, do ye even so to them: for this is the law and the prophets."*
>
> Matthew 7:12 (KJV)

Prayer

Dear Heavenly Father, I beg of you to teach my child to have respect for those around them, whether or not they are family, a friend, or anyone else that they care for. Please teach my child that respect and kindness are for everyone, not for selected people. Guide my child into showing everyone love and empathy because that is the person you plan for them to be. Amen.

Reflection Question

How can you teach your child to value and respect the feelings and perspectives of others? What are some practical ways your child can demonstrate kindness in their relationships?

Prayer for Romantic Relationships

> *"Be ye not unequally yoked together with unbelievers: for what fellowship hath righteousness with unrighteousness? and what communion hath light with darkness?"*
>
> 2 Corinthians 6:14 (KJV)

Prayer

Dear Almighty Father, please guide my child as they go off on their own romantic endeavors. Please guide my child into relationships that would honor You. Please guide my child into taking their time, whether it be in choosing their partner, going on to the next steps in their relationship, or even considering if they should cease the romantic relationship. Guide them into being a respectful and God-honoring romantic partner. Amen.

Reflection Question

How can you help your child establish healthy boundaries and expectations in romantic relationships? How can your child prioritize their faith and values when considering a romantic partner?

4
PRAYING FOR YOUR CHILD'S FUTURE

Prayer for Guidance

> *"Trust in the LORD with all thine heart; and lean not unto thine own understanding. In all thy ways acknowledge him, and he shall direct thy paths."*
>
> Proverbs 3:5-6 (KJV)

Prayer

Dear God, I ask you to grant guidance unto my child. Guide them towards the purpose You have planned for them from before they were born. Allow them to seek Your counsel in all decisions they must make from now and for the rest of their lives. Give them clarity and wisdom so they may do only what honors You. Amen.

Reflection Question

How can you trust in God's guidance for your child's future? What steps can your child take to seek God's will in their decision-making?

Prayer for Wisdom

> *"If any of you lack wisdom, let him ask of God, that giveth to all men liberally, and upbraideth not; and it shall be given him."*
>
> James 1:5 (KJV)

Prayer

Dear Holy Father, I pray that You give my child wisdom and a clear heart and mind. Please fill them with understanding and compassion so that they may continue to make choices that are wise, helpful, and beneficial to those around them, and that would honor You. Please also have them use their wisdom for good. Amen.

Reflection Question

How can your child seek God's wisdom in their academic and personal pursuits? In what areas of their life do they need wisdom for the future?

Prayer for Protection

> *"For he shall give his angels charge over thee, to keep thee in all thy ways."*
>
> Psalm 91:11 (KJV)

Prayer

Dear Heavenly God, I pray that You protect my child from all the evil that comes with living in Your world. Keep my child away from temptation and shield them from those that intend to do them harm. Keep them safe so that they may continue to continue spreading the word of Your love and so that they may grow into the person You plan for them to be. Amen.

Reflection Question

How can you trust in God's protection for your child's future? What steps can your child take to stay away from harmful influences?

Prayer for Purpose

> *"For we are his workmanship, created in Christ Jesus unto good works, which God hath before ordained that we should walk in them."*
>
> Ephesians 2:10 (KJV)

Prayer

Dear Almighty God, I pray You help my child find the purpose You intend for them soon. Allow them the glory and grace of knowing their life's purpose so that they may spend the rest of their days using their purpose, their gifts, and their passions to spread Your word and the grace of Your love. Amen.

Reflection Question

How can you help your child discover their God-given gifts and talents? In what ways can your child use their abilities to serve others and bring glory to God?

Prayer for Strength and Perseverance

"I can do all things through Christ which strengtheneth me."

Philippians 4:13 (KJV)

Prayer

Dear God, I pray for You to grant strength unto my child. Grant them strength so that they will be able to keep track of their goals. Give them strength so that they can continue to reject evil and temptation. Give them strength so that they can continue spreading the word of Your love to all those around them. Amen.

Reflection Question

How can your child rely on God's strength during difficult times? What are some strategies your child can use to stay determined and focused on their goals?

Prayer for Faith and Trust

> *"Trust in the LORD with all thine heart; and lean not unto thine own understanding. In all thy ways acknowledge him, and he shall direct thy paths."*
>
> Proverbs 3:5-6 (KJV)

Prayer

Dear God, as my child continues to grow and develop, I pray You deepen their faith in You. I pray You keep them on the path You intended for them so that they do not stray. I pray that they continue to spread the word of Your love and keep true to their faith in You. Amen.

Reflection Question

How can your child develop a stronger faith in God's provision for their future? What can they do to cultivate trust in God's timing?

Prayer for Opportunities

> *"Ask, and it shall be given you; seek, and ye shall find; knock, and it shall be opened unto you."*
>
> Matthew 7:7 (KJV)

Prayer

Dear God, I pray that You not only guide my child but open doors and opportunities for them so that they may grow into the person you plan for them to be. Continue to guide my child towards new experiences so that they may go through whatever you have to offer them and so that they may grow with Your wisdom, love, and enlightenment. Amen.

Reflection Question

How can your child actively seek and recognize opportunities that come their way? How can they discern if an opportunity aligns with God's plan for their future?

Prayer for Contentment

> *"Not that I speak in respect of want: for I have learned, in whatsoever state I am, therewith to be content."*
>
> Philippians 4:11 (KJV)

Prayer

Dear Heavenly God, I pray You teach my child to count their blessings. I pray for my child to learn the value of being content with what they already have and to be grateful for them. I pray You help them find joy and happiness with the simplicities of life so that they may forever be grateful to You and Your wonders. Amen.

Reflection Question

How can your child cultivate a heart of contentment amidst the uncertainties of the future? What steps can they take to find joy and fulfillment in their current circumstances?

5
PRAYING FOR YOUR CHILD'S EDUCATION

Prayer for Academic Success

"For the LORD giveth wisdom: out of his mouth cometh knowledge and understanding."

Proverbs 2:6 (KJV)

Prayer

Dear Holy God, I pray that you bless my child with the ability to learn quickly and easily. I pray that You guide them so that they may use their knowledge effectively for the people around them. Please help them to do well in their academic pursuits so that it may open bigger and better doors for them in the future. Amen.

Reflection Question

How can you support your child's academic growth and development? In what ways can your child cultivate a love for learning?

Prayer for Wisdom

> *"Happy is the man that findeth wisdom and the man that getteth understanding."*
>
> Proverbs 3:13 (KJV)

Prayer

Dear Holy God, please grant my child the wisdom for their academic success. Give them the wisdom to prioritize their school work, give them the wisdom to focus on their studies, and give them the wisdom to make choices that would be beneficial to their academic pursuits. Keep them away from temptation, please, O Lord. Amen.

Reflection Question

How can your child seek wisdom in their studies and decision-making? In what ways can you model and encourage wise choices in your child's education?

Prayer for Focus and Concentration

> *"Let thine eyes look right on, and let thine eyelids look straight before thee."*
>
> Proverbs 4:25 (KJV)

Prayer

O Dear Holy God, I pray that you keep my child focused on their studies. I pray that You ensure their attention is always to thrive for their academic success. Please, Lord, grant them the ability to learn quickly and effectively in school, homework, and any extracurriculars they may have. Amen.

Reflection Question

How can your child develop healthy study habits and routines? What distractions can your child minimize to enhance their focus and concentration?

Prayer for Guidance in Choosing the Right Path

"I will instruct thee and teach thee in the way which thou shalt go: I will guide thee with mine eye."

Psalm 32:8 (KJV)

Prayer

Dear God, I pray that you guide my child into choosing the path they believe to be best for their academic future. Please guide them so that they may choose the path that both honors You and will allow them to strive for the best that they can in their educational pursuits. Please mentor them in this so that they may also use their success to spread the word of Your love. Amen.

Reflection Question

How can your child seek God's guidance in their educational decisions? In what ways can you support and provide guidance to your child in their educational journey?

Prayer for Character Development

"Seest thou a man diligent in his business? he shall stand before kings; he shall not stand before mean men."

Proverbs 22:29 (KJV)

Prayer

Dear Heavenly God, I pray that you guide my child into staying kind, humble, and compassionate no matter how much success and confidence they are able to gain through their achievements. Allow them to continue being a person others can come to for help and to feel Your love. Keep them full of diligence, humility, perseverance, and integrity. Amen.

Reflection Question

How can your child develop character traits that will benefit their educational journey and future endeavors? How can you encourage and model virtues of diligence, humility, perseverance, and integrity in my child's education?

Prayer for Favorable Learning Environments

> *"He that walketh with wise men shall be wise: but a companion of fools shall be destroyed."*
>
> Proverbs 13:20 (KJV)

Prayer

Dear God, I pray that you provide my child with a learning environment where they can be most productive. Please allow them to have peers and teachers who will help them grow to be the best student they can be. Please give them peers who value education just as much as they do and teachers who will keep them safe and teach them properly. Amen.

Reflection Question

How can you advocate for a positive and conducive learning environment for your child? How can your child choose friends and study groups that positively impact their educational journey?

Prayer for Overcoming Challenges

"I can do all things through Christ which strengtheneth me."

Philippians 4:13 (KJV)

Prayer

Dear Holy God, give my child the strength and courage that they need in order to overcome any academic challenges that come their way. Please give them all the help You are able to give them so that they may continue to strive for excellence. Allow them Your love so that they may use the value of their education to continue spreading Your word. Amen.

Reflection Question

How can your child develop a mindset of resilience and perseverance in their educational pursuits? What strategies can your child use to overcome challenges and setbacks in their studies?

Prayer for a Love of Truth and Knowledge

> "The heart of the prudent getteth knowledge; and the ear of the wise seeketh knowledge."
>
> Proverbs 18:15 (KJV)

Prayer

Dear Heavenly God, I pray that you plant a love of learning and a thirst for knowledge in my child. Allow them to feed that love and thirst so that they may continue to learn all about the world and universe that You have created. Keep them wanting to learn more, even if it is outside of the classroom. Amen.

Reflection Question

How can your child develop a love for truth and knowledge that extends beyond the classroom? What opportunities can you provide to foster a spirit of lifelong learning in your child?

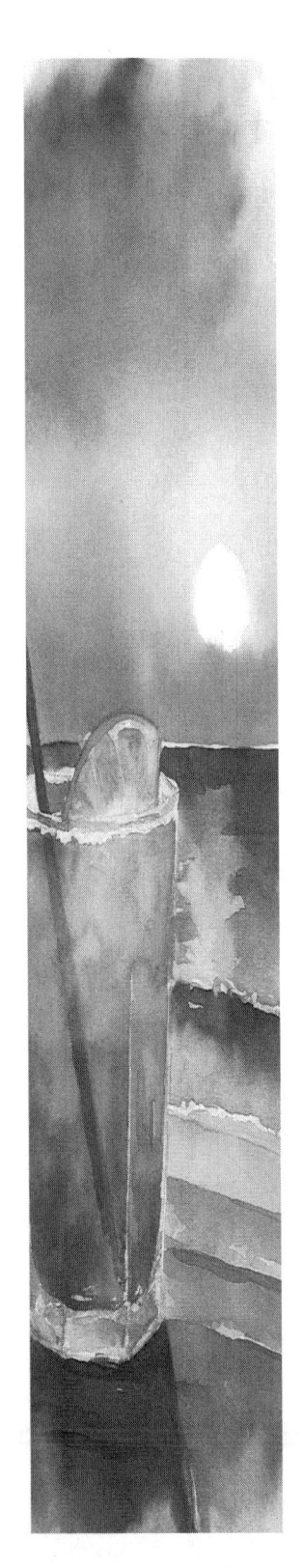

6
PRAYING FOR YOUR CHILD'S EMOTIONAL WELL-BEING

Prayer for Inner Peace

> *"And the peace of God, which passeth all understanding, shall keep your hearts and minds through Christ Jesus."*
>
> Philippians 4:7 (KJV)

Prayer

Dear Holy God, I pray that You grant my child a calm mind and a peaceful demeanor when they are faced with the challenges of life. I pray that you help them calm their anxieties and worries so that they may keep a clear mind to overcome them. I pray that you fill them with calmness and serenity. Amen.

Reflection Question

How can you create an environment of peace and tranquility for your child? What practices can your child adopt to cultivate inner peace in their daily life?

Prayer for Joy and Happiness

"Thou wilt shew me the path of life: in thy presence is fullness of joy; at thy right hand there are pleasures for evermore."

Psalm 16:11 (KJV)

Prayer

Dear Heavenly Father, I pray that you help my child gain a heart that is filled with genuine happiness and joy. I pray that you allow them to find delight in the simplest things of life and that they are grateful for the smallest of blessings. Allow them to see the beauty of Your creation and to appreciate it. Amen.

Reflection Question

How can you cultivate an atmosphere of joy and positivity in your home? What activities or hobbies bring genuine joy to your child's heart?

Prayer for Emotional Healing

"He healeth the broken in heart, and bindeth up their wounds."

Psalm 147:3 (KJV)

Prayer

Dear Almighty Father, I pray that you help my child heal their heart emotionally. Please help them to soothe the pain away from their innermost feelings so that my child can continue to be happy, joyful, and full of smiles and laughter as they grow in Your peaceful and loving arms. Amen.

Reflection Question

How can you create a safe space for your child to express and process their emotions? What steps can your child take toward emotional healing and wholeness?

Prayer for Self-Acceptance

"I will praise thee; for I am fearfully and wonderfully made: marvelous are thy works; and that my soul knoweth right well."

Psalm 139:14 (KJV)

Prayer

Dear Lord, I pray that you allow my child to see the beauty in their own uniqueness and individuality. teach them the value of their worth so that they may not ever allow anyone to take advantage of them. Teach them to love themselves for their oddities and those around them because we are all made in Your perfect image. Amen.

Reflection Question

How can you foster a healthy sense of self-esteem and self-acceptance in your child? What affirmations or practices can help your child recognize their inherent worth?

Prayer for Emotional Resilience

> "My brethren, count it all joy when ye fall into divers temptations; Knowing this, that the trying of your faith worketh patience. But let patience have her perfect work, that ye may be perfect and entire, wanting nothing."
>
> James 1:2-4 (KJV)

Prayer

Dear Heavenly Father, I pray that you help my child strengthen their emotions so that they may not be easily hurt. Allow them to take any pain and turn it into love instead. Teach them to control their emotions so that they do not easily react based on their feelings but rather with a calm mind and a loving and forgiving heart. Amen.

Reflection Question

How can you teach your child to develop emotional resilience and bounce back from challenges? What strategies can your child implement to maintain a positive mindset in difficult situations?

Prayer for Emotional Balance

"A fool uttereth all his mind: but a wise man keepeth it in till afterwards."

Proverbs 29:11 (KJV)

Prayer

Dear God, I pray that you grant my child the ability to keep their emotions balanced and stable. Allow them to find a healthy method of controlling and balancing their emotions so that they may not harm themselves or others. Allow them the strength to express and regulate their feelings in a calm and productive manner. Amen.

Reflection Question

How can you teach my child to recognize and express their emotions in a healthy manner? What coping mechanisms can your child develop to regulate their emotions during challenging times?

Prayer for Empathy and Compassion

> *"Finally, be ye all of one mind, having compassion for one of another, love as brethren, be pitiful, be courteous."*
>
> 1 Peter 3:8 (KJV)

Prayer

Dear Almighty Father, I ask you to give my child a heart that is full of empathy and compassion. Please allow them to find ways to help others in need. Give them the strength and wisdom needed for them to be able to spread your love through helping others and having compassion for them. Amen.

Reflection Question

How can you encourage your child to develop empathy towards others' emotions? What actions can your child take to show compassion and support to those in need?

Prayer for Gratitude

> *"In everything give thanks: for this is the will of God in Christ Jesus concerning you."*
>
> 1 Thessalonians 5:18 (KJV)

Prayer

Dear Heavenly God, I pray that you teach my child how to be grateful for all of the things they have in their life. Please help them recognize and appreciate all of the blessings that they already have in their life. Please also grant them the wisdom and compassion to share their blessings with others. Amen.

Reflection Question

How can you cultivate an attitude of gratitude in your child's life? What practices can your child adopt to express gratitude for the blessings they receive? How can you encourage your child to develop empathy towards others' emotions? What actions can your child take to show compassion and support to those in need?

ENCOURAGEMENT TO CONTINUE PRAYING

Teaching children how to pray from a very young age is one of the most important things a parent could do for their child during their early years. A child already learning how to pray would make it easier for the child to grow up to be faithful to God and His teachings. Being faithful to God is more than simply just asking for His guidance, wisdom, love, and care; it also comes with hard work. God can give you the ability to do anything you ask for, but it is also up to the child to keep in mind that all the hard work is up to them.

In this book, prayers that touch on all kinds of topics regarding children are provided to make it easier for the child to pray. Hopefully, with regular usage of the prayers in this book, the child would, later on, be able to come up with their own prayers that are made in their own words that would better suit their needs. One must, however, understand that prayer is not the complete answer to their wants and needs. With prayer comes the actual action. If one were to ask God for wisdom, one must also actively remind themselves to think for themselves because the answer will not magically come to them. It is important to remind children of this very fact.

Along with prayers that children could use, this book also provides prayers that parents and guardians would also be able to use when they would like to say a prayer for their children. Parents can pray for academic success for their children with the help of this book. A parent can also pray for the health and well-being of their child, that they may be healed from their sickness, or that sickness never comes unto them at all. Parents can also pray for their children to be given wisdom and guidance so that they may stay focused and learn to reject temptation.

However, just like with children, parents must also understand that they, too, must do the work. It is also up to the parents and guardians to teach their children how to be good, kind, loving, and understanding in the image that God intended for them to have. It is important that parents show all of the things they would like their child to portray so that their children would have good role models to model themselves after.

With this book, parents and children can pray together. A parent can even teach their child how to pray by praying along with them. Seeing their parents pray alongside them will not only encourage a child to pray with their parents, but it will also encourage them to pray in their own time or by themselves, even without the help or command of their parents. Parents must lead by example, and by showing their children that they too are full of faith, their child shall also follow their lead.

Colossians 3:21 (KJV)

"Fathers, provoke not your children to anger, lest they be discouraged."

THANK YOU
for your purchase!

Grow your faith with a **free** bonus book included in *every* purchase.

GET IT NOW

Every purchase comes with a free bonus book download.

FAITH LABS

ABOUT US

FaithLabs is a faith-based publisher dedicated to producing books that inspire and uplift readers.

With a focus on Christian values and principles, FaithLab's team of experienced editors work closely with authors to bring their messages of hope and faith to life. From devotional books to inspirational memoirs, FaithLabs offers a range of titles to deepen reader's spiritual journeys.

Thanks for reading,

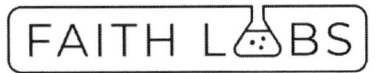

FAITH LABS

REVIEW CLUB

Your Voice Matters

YOU'RE INVITED!

1. LEAVE A QUICK REVIEW OF THE BOOK

   USA | CANADA | UK | AUSTRALIA

2. DOWNLOAD EACH WEEK'S FREE KINDLE BOOK

3. THAT'S IT!

www.kindlepromos.com/club

FAITH LABS · kindlepromos

Made in the USA
Middletown, DE
09 March 2025